Rubs & Seasonings

Recipes to make your own gifts

Use these recipes to delight your friends and family. Each recipe includes gift tags for your convenience – just cut them out and personalize!

After personalizing your tag, fold and attach it to the top of the bag (above the sealed strip). Attach the tag with staples, or for a more decorative gift in a bag, use raffia, ribbon, twine, yarn or string. To do this, punch one or more holes in the top of your bag and tag at the same time. Then secure the tag using the raffia, ribbon, twine, yarn or string.

These gifts should keep for up to six months.

D0980978

Printed in the United States of America
by G&R Publishing Co.

Distributed By:

507 Industrial Street
Waverly, IA 50677

ISBN 1-56383-141-4
Item #3530

Rajin' Cajun Rub Mix

1 T. plus 1 1/2 tsp. dried basil
1 T. plus 1 1/2 tsp. dried oregano
1 T. plus 1 1/2 tsp. paprika
1 T. plus 1 1/2 tsp. salt
1 T. dried thyme
1 1/2 tsp. allspice

Combine the above ingredients and stir until well blended. Place in a 3" x 4" ziplock bag and seal.

Attach a gift tag with the directions on how to use the rub.

Ragin' Cajun Rub

Ragin' Cajun Rub Mix
Beef or pork

Sprinkle and rub the mix according to taste preferences over both sides of beef or pork before grilling, broiling, baking or frying.

Ragin' Cajun Rub

Ragin' Cajun Rub Mix
Beef or pork

Sprinkle and rub the mix according to taste preferences over both sides of beef or pork before grilling, broiling, baking or frying.

★ Grilling Tip ★

Never use alcohol, gasoline or kerosene as a lighter fluid starter — all three can cause an explosion.

- - - - - - - - - -fold- - - - - - - - -

Ragin' Cajun Rub

Ragin' Cajun Rub Mix
Beef or pork

Sprinkle and rub the mix according to taste preferences over both sides of beef or pork before grilling, broiling, baking or frying.

★ Grilling Tip ★

To get a sluggish charcoal grill going, place two or three additional coals in a small metal can and add lighter fluid. Then stack them on the coals in the grill and light.

- - - - - - - - - - fold - - - - - - - - - -

Robust Spaghetti Sauce Seasoning Mix

1 whole clove
1 1/2 tsp. dried oregano
1/2 tsp. dried rosemary
1 bay leaf
1 1/2 tsp. dried basil

1 1/2 tsp. black pepper
1/2 tsp. sugar
2 T. dried parsley

Combine the above ingredients and stir until well blended. Place in a 3" x 4" ziplock bag and seal.

Attach a gift tag with the directions on how to use the seasoning.

Robust Spaghetti Sauce

1 pkg. Robust Spaghetti Sauce
    Seasoning Mix
1 to 2 (29 oz.) cans tomato sauce, 1 to 2
    (29 oz.) cans crushed tomatoes or 10
    to 15 large tomatoes, skinned and
    crushed
Crushed garlic to taste
Salt to taste

    In saucepan combine tomatoes, seasoning mix and garlic. Bring to a boil then reduce to simmer. Simmer to desired consistency. Salt to taste before serving.

Robust Spaghetti Sauce

1 pkg. Robust Spaghetti   Crushed garlic to taste
     Sauce Seasoning Mix   Salt to taste
1 to 2 (29 oz.) cans tomato sauce, 1 to 2 (29 oz.) cans
    crushed tomatoes or 10 to 15 large tomatoes,
    skinned and crushed

    In saucepan combine tomatoes, seasoning mix and
garlic. Bring to a boil then reduce to simmer. Simmer to
desired consistency. Salt to taste before serving.

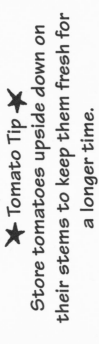

★ Tomato Tip ★
Store tomatoes upside down on
their stems to keep them fresh for
a longer time.

- - - - fold - - - -

Robust Spaghetti Sauce

1 pkg. Robust Spaghetti
Sauce Seasoning Mix
1 to 2 (29 oz.) cans tomato sauce, 1 to 2 (29 oz.) cans
crushed tomatoes or 10 to 15 large tomatoes,
skinned and crushed

Crushed garlic to taste
Salt to taste

In saucepan combine tomatoes, seasoning mix and
garlic. Bring to a boil then reduce to simmer. Simmer to
desired consistency. Salt to taste before serving.

Pasta Tip

Use at least one quart of water for every four ounces of dry pasta. Add pasta to boiling water. Cook pasta, uncovered, at a fast boil.

- - - - fold - - - - - - - - - -

Oriental Marinade Mix

1 T. anise
1 T. fennel
1 T. ground ginger
1 T. garlic powder
1 tsp. black pepper

Combine the above ingredients and stir until well blended. Place in a 3" x 4" ziplock bag and seal.

Attach a gift tag with the directions on how to use the marinade.

Oriental Marinade

1 pkg. Oriental Marinade Mix
1/2 C. soy sauce
Beef, pork, chicken or turkey

To prepare, combine Oriental Marinade Mix with soy sauce and marinate beef, pork, chicken or turkey for 1 to 2 hours before grilling, broiling, baking or frying.

Oriental Marinade

1 pkg. Oriental Marinade Mix
1/2 C. soy sauce
Beef, pork, chicken or turkey

To prepare, combine Oriental Marinade Mix with soy sauce and marinate beef, pork, chicken or turkey for 1 to 2 hours before grilling, broiling, baking or frying.

★ Grilling Tip ★

To light a charcoal fire, arrange 20 to 30 coals in a pyramid shape. Soak the coals with about 1/2 cup lighter fluid, wait 1 minute for the fluid to soak into the coals and then light with a match.

- - - - - - - fold - - - - - - -

Oriental Marinade

1 pkg. Oriental Marinade Mix
1/2 C. soy sauce
Beef, pork, chicken or turkey

To prepare, combine Oriental Marinade Mix with soy sauce and marinate beef, pork, chicken or turkey for 1 to 2 hours before grilling, broiling, baking or frying.

★ Grilling Tip ★
Always use tongs or a spatula when handling meat. Avoid piercing the meat with a fork.

- - - - - - - - - - - fold - - - - - - - - - - -

All South BBQ Rub Mix

1 1/2 tsp. garlic salt   1 1/2 tsp. chili powder
1 1/2 tsp. sugar   1 1/2 tsp. black pepper
1 1/2 tsp. brown sugar   3/4 tsp. cayenne pepper
1 1/2 tsp. cumin seed   1 T. paprika

Combine the above ingredients and stir until well blended. Place in a 3" x 4" ziplock bag and seal.

Attach a gift tag with the directions on how to use the rub.

❀ *Fill a gift basket with rub mixes, grilling tools, a grill brush and an apron.* ❀

All South BBQ Rub

All South BBQ Rub Mix
Beef, pork, chicken or turkey

Sprinkle and rub the mix according to taste preferences on both sides of beef, pork, chicken or turkey before grilling, broiling, baking or frying.

All South BBQ Rub

All South BBQ Rub Mix
Beef, pork, chicken or turkey

Sprinkle and rub the mix according to taste preferences on both sides of beef, pork, chicken or turkey before grilling, broiling, baking or frying.

★ Grilling Tip ★

To keep a grill rack or grid clean, scrub the grid with a stiff brush while it is still warm.

- - - - fold - - - - - - - -

All South BBQ Rub

All South BBQ Rub Mix
Beef, pork, chicken or turkey

Sprinkle and rub the mix according to taste preferences on both sides of beef, pork, chicken or turkey before grilling, broiling, baking or frying.

★ Broiling Tip ★
When broiling meat, cover your pan
with tin foil and place meat
directly on foil. This will make
clean up much easier.

- - - - - - - - - - fold- - - - - - - - - -

Pork Roast Rub Mix

2 T. garlic salt
2 T. black pepper
1 T. dried sage
1 T. paprika
1 1/2 tsp. dry mustard

Combine the above ingredients and stir until well blended. Place in a 3" x 4" ziplock bag and seal.

Attach a gift tag with the directions on how to use the rub.

Pork Roast Rub

Pork Roast Rub Mix
Pork roast

Sprinkle and rub the mix according to taste preferences on all sides of roast before baking.

Pork Roast Rub

Pork Roast Rub Mix
Pork roast

Sprinkle and rub the mix according to taste
preferences on all sides of roast before baking.

★ Broiling Tip ★
When broiling meat, trim excess
fat to prevent flare-ups
in your oven.

- - - - - - fold - - - - - - - - -

Pork Roast Rub

Pork Roast Rub Mix
Pork roast

Sprinkle and rub the mix according to taste
preferences on all sides of roast before baking.

★ Grilling Tip ★

When grilling, baking or broiling meat, allow meat to rest for about 5 minutes before serving. This allows for the meat to finish cooking and for juices to settle throughout the meat.

- - - - - - - fold- - - - - - - - -

Lemon Kick Rub Mix

4 T. lemon pepper
2 T. plus 1 1/2 tsp. seasoning salt
1 T. plus 1 1/2 tsp. garlic powder

Combine the above ingredients and stir until well blended. Place in a 3" x 4" ziplock bag and seal.

Attach a gift tag with the directions on how to use the rub.

❀ *For a fun gift, put three or four different rub mixes into an oven mitt.* ❀

Lemon Kick Rub

Lemon Kick Rub Mix
Fish, chicken or turkey

Sprinkle and rub the mix according to taste preferences on both sides of fish, chicken or turkey before grilling, broiling, baking or frying.

Lemon Kick Rub

Lemon Kick Rub Mix
Fish, chicken or turkey

Sprinkle and rub the mix according to taste preferences on both sides of fish, chicken or turkey before grilling, broiling, baking or frying.

★ Grilling Tip ★

Before grilling, remove grill rack and lightly spray or coat with vegetable oil or cooking spray to keep food from sticking. This holds especially true for fish.

- - - - - - fold - - - - - - - -

Lemon Kick Rub

Lemon Kick Rub Mix
Fish, chicken or turkey

Sprinkle and rub the mix according to taste preferences on both sides of fish, chicken or turkey before grilling, broiling, baking or frying.

★ Grilling Tip ★

When using a charcoal grill, knock off white ash before putting food on the grill by shaking the grill or tapping coals with a utensil. This prevents the food from tasting like charcoal.

-- -- -- -- fold-- -- -- -- --

Pot Roast Rub Mix

2 T. beef bouillon granules
2 T. minced onion
1 T. garlic salt
1 T. seasoning salt
1 T. dried rosemary
1 T. black pepper

Combine the above ingredients and stir until well blended. Place in a 3" x 4" ziplock bag and seal.

Attach a gift tag with the directions on how to use the rub.

Pot Roast Rub

Pot Roast Rub Mix
Beef roast

Sprinkle and rub the mix according to taste preferences on all sides of beef before baking.

Pot Roast Rub

Pot Roast Rub Mix
Beef roast

Sprinkle and rub the mix according to taste
preferences on all sides of beef before baking.

★ Grilling Tip ★

When grilling, get the grill rack very hot before placing food on the grill. The food will then sear, lock in natural juices and cook evenly. The food will cook faster and taste better.

- - - - - - - - - fold - - - - - - - - - -

Pot Roast Rub

Pot Roast Rub Mix
Beef roast

Sprinkle and rub the mix according to taste
preferences on all sides of beef before baking.

★ Grilling Tip ★

When grilling, to determine how hot the fire is, hold your hand above it and start counting. If you have to pull away on the count of one, the fire is very hot, on the count of three, the fire is medium hot and on the count of five, the fire is low.

- - - - - - - - - - fold - - - - - - - - - -

Tex-Mex Rub Mix

2 T. chili powder
2 T. cumin
1 T. onion salt
1 T. garlic salt
1 1/2 tsp. ground oregano

Combine the above ingredients and stir until well blended. Place in a 3" x 4" ziplock bag and seal.

Attach a gift tag with the directions on how to use the rub.

Tex-Mex Rub

Tex-Mex Rub Mix
Beef or pork

Sprinkle and rub the mix according to taste preferences on both sides of beef or pork before grilling, broiling, baking or frying.

Tex-Mex Rub

Tex-Mex Rub Mix
Beef or pork

Sprinkle and rub the mix according to taste preferences on both sides of beef or pork before grilling, broiling, baking or frying.

★ Grilling Tip ★

When grilling, chicken and turkey should be cooked over low heat for slow, covered cooking.

- - - - - - fold - - - - - -

Tex-Mex Rub

Tex-Mex Rub Mix
Beef or pork

Sprinkle and rub the mix according to taste preferences on both sides of beef or pork before grilling, broiling, baking or frying.

★ Grilling Tip ★

When grilling, remember air temperature affects cooking time. On colder days your food will take longer to grill. Keep the lid on until you're ready to cook. Every time the lid is opened, you extend the cooking time.

- - - - - - - - fold - - - - - - - - - - - - -

Greek Seasoning Rub Mix

1 T. salt
1 T. dried oregano
2 1/4 tsp. onion powder
2 1/4 tsp. garlic powder
1 1/2 tsp. cornstarch
1 1/2 tsp. black pepper

1 1/2 tsp. beef
   bouillon granules
1 1/2 tsp. dried parsley
3/4 tsp. ground cinnamon
3/4 tsp. ground nutmeg

Combine the above ingredients and stir until well blended. Place in a 3" x 4" ziplock bag and seal.

Attach a gift tag with the directions on how to use the rub.

Greek Seasoning Rub

Greek Seasoning Rub Mix
Beef, pork, chicken or turkey

Sprinkle and rub the mix according to taste preferences on both sides of beef, pork, chicken or turkey before grilling, broiling, baking or frying.

Greek Seasoning Rub

Greek Seasoning Rub Mix
Beef, pork, chicken or turkey

Sprinkle and rub the mix according to taste preferences on both sides of beef, pork, chicken or turkey before grilling, broiling, baking or frying.

★ Grilling Tip ★

When grilling, steaks and chops should be turned over when juices appear on their top surface. Peek underneath and make sure the color is golden brown before turning.

- - - - - - - - - -fold- - - - - - - - - -

Greek Seasoning Rub

Greek Seasoning Rub Mix
Beef, pork, chicken or turkey

Sprinkle and rub the mix according to taste preferences on both sides of beef, pork, chicken or turkey before grilling, broiling, baking or frying.

★ Grilling Tip ★

When grilling, it is usually best to turn the meat only once. When grilling meat to a medium or greater doneness, use the lid to assist in cooking. This will decrease the cooking time by applying heat to all sides of the meat at once.

- - - - - - fold- - - - - - - - - - -

Herb Bouquet Rub Mix

1 1/8 tsp. black pepper
2 1/4 tsp. dry mustard
2 1/4 tsp. dried rosemary
1 T. plus 3/4 tsp. dried oregano
1 T. plus 3/4 tsp. dried thyme

Combine the above ingredients and stir until well blended. Place in a 3" x 4" ziplock bag and seal.

Attach a gift tag with the directions on how to use the rub.

Herb Bouquet Rub

Herb Bouquet Rub Mix
Fish, beef, pork, chicken or turkey

Sprinkle and rub the mix according to taste preferences on both sides of fish, beef, pork, chicken or turkey before grilling, broiling, baking or frying.

Herb Bouquet Rub

Herb Bouquet Rub Mix
Fish, beef, pork, chicken or turkey

Sprinkle and rub the mix according to taste preferences on both sides of fish, beef, pork, chicken or turkey before grilling, broiling, baking or frying.

★ Grilling Tip ★

When grilling steaks or chops, choose cuts that are at least 1 inch thick for tender, moist and tasty steaks and chops.

- - - - - - - fold - - - - - - - -

Herb Bouquet Rub

Herb Bouquet Rub Mix
Fish, beef, pork, chicken or turkey

Sprinkle and rub the mix according to taste preferences on both sides of fish, beef, pork, chicken or turkey before grilling, broiling, baking or frying.

★ Grilling Tip ★
When grilling, place food about 3/4" apart for even cooking.

- - - - - - fold - - - - - - -

BBQ Spice Rub Mix

1 T. paprika	3/4 tsp. dry mustard
1 1/2 tsp. chili powder	3/4 tsp. black pepper
1 1/2 tsp. cumin	3/4 tsp. dried thyme
1 1/2 tsp. coriander	3/4 tsp. curry powder
1 1/2 tsp. sugar	3/4 tsp. cayenne pepper
1 1/2 tsp. salt	

Combine the above ingredients and stir until well blended. Place in a 3" x 4" ziplock bag and seal.

Attach a gift tag with the directions on how to use the rub.

BBQ Spice Rub

BBQ Spice Rub Mix
Beef or pork

Sprinkle and rub the mix according to taste preferences on both sides of beef or pork before grilling, broiling, baking or frying.

BBQ Spice Rub

BBQ Spice Rub Mix
Beef or pork

Sprinkle and rub the mix according to taste preferences on both sides of beef or pork before grilling, broiling, baking or frying.

⭐ Grilling Tip ⭐

Never use alcohol, gasoline or kerosene as a lighter fluid starter – all three can cause an explosion.

- - - - - - - - - - - - -fold- - - - - - - - - -

BBQ Spice Rub

BBQ Spice Rub Mix
Beef or pork

Sprinkle and rub the mix according to taste preferences on both sides of beef or pork before grilling, broiling, baking or frying.

Grilling Tip

Keep a water bottle handy to mist any flare-ups on charcoal grills. For gas grills, reduce the temperature.

- - - - - - - - fold - - - - - - - - - -

Orleans Pepper Rub Mix

2 T. plus 1 1/2 tsp. cayenne pepper
1 T. plus 1 1/2 tsp. black pepper
2 T. plus 1 1/2 tsp. onion powder
1 T. plus 1 1/2 tsp. salt

Combine the above ingredients and stir until well blended. Place in a 3" x 4" ziplock bag and seal.

Attach a gift tag with the directions on how to use the rub.

Orleans Pepper Rub

Orleans Pepper Rub Mix
Beef, pork, chicken or turkey

Sprinkle and rub the mix according to taste preferences on both sides of beef, pork, chicken or turkey before grilling, broiling, baking or frying.

Orleans Pepper Rub

Orleans Pepper Rub Mix
Beef, pork, chicken or turkey

Sprinkle and rub the mix according to taste preferences on both sides of beef, pork, chicken or turkey before grilling, broiling, baking or frying.

★ Grilling Tip ★
To keep a grill rack or grid clean, scrub the grid with a stiff brush while it is still warm.

- - - - - - - - - fold - - - - - - - - -

Orleans Pepper Rub

Orleans Pepper Rub Mix
Beef, pork, chicken or turkey

Sprinkle and rub the mix according to taste preferences on both sides of beef, pork, chicken or turkey before grilling, broiling, baking or frying.

★ Grilling Tip ★

Always use tongs or a spatula when handling meat. Avoid piercing the meat with a fork.

- - - - - - fold - - - - - - - - -

Cucina Italia Rub Mix

2 T. plus 1 1/2 tsp. dried oregano
2 T. plus 1 1/2 tsp. dried basil
1 T. plus 1 1/2 tsp. garlic powder
1 T. plus 1 1/2 tsp. salt

Combine the above ingredients and stir until well blended. Place in a 3" x 4" ziplock bag and seal.

Attach a gift tag with the directions on how to use the rub.

Cucina Italia Rub

Cucina Italia Rub Mix
Beef, pork, chicken or turkey

Sprinkle and rub the mix according to taste preferences on both sides of beef, pork, chicken or turkey before grilling, broiling, baking or frying.

Cucina Italia Rub

Cucina Italia Rub Mix
Beef, pork, chicken or turkey

Sprinkle and rub the mix according to taste
preferences on both sides of beef, pork, chicken or turkey
before grilling, broiling, baking or frying.

⭐ Grilling Tip ⭐

Before grilling, remove grill rack and lightly spray or coat with vegetable oil or cooking spray to keep food from sticking. This holds especially true for fish.

- - - - - - fold - - - - - - -

Cucina Italia Rub

Cucina Italia Rub Mix
Beef, pork, chicken or turkey

Sprinkle and rub the mix according to taste preferences on both sides of beef, pork, chicken or turkey before grilling, broiling, baking or frying.

★ Grilling Tip ★

To get a sluggish charcoal grill going, place two or three additional coals in a small metal can and add lighter fluid. Then stack them on the coals in the grill and light.

- - - - - fold - - - - - - -

Mexican Seasoning Rub Mix

4 T. chili powder
2 1/4 tsp. ground cumin
2 1/4 tsp. dried oregano
2 1/4 tsp. garlic powder
2 1/4 tsp. salt
1/2 tsp. ground cloves

Combine the above ingredients and stir until well blended. Place in a 3" x 4" ziplock bag and seal.

Attach a gift tag with the directions on how to use the rub.

Mexican Seasoning Rub

Mexican Seasoning Rub Mix
Beef, pork, chicken or turkey

Sprinkle and rub the mix according to taste preferences on both sides of beef, pork, chicken or turkey before grilling, broiling, baking or frying.

Mexican Seasoning Rub

Mexican Seasoning Rub Mix
Beef, pork, chicken or turkey

Sprinkle and rub the mix according to taste preferences on both sides of beef, pork, chicken or turkey before grilling, broiling, baking or frying.

★ Grilling Tip ★

When using a charcoal grill, the number of coals required for grilling depends on the size and type of grill and the amount of food to be prepared. As a general rule, it takes about 30 coals to grill 1 pound of meat.

- - - - - - - - - - - - fold - - - - - - - - - - - -

Mexican Seasoning Rub

Mexican Seasoning Rub Mix
Beef, pork, chicken or turkey

Sprinkle and rub the mix according to taste preferences on both sides of beef, pork, chicken or turkey before grilling, broiling, baking or frying.

★ Grilling Tip ★

When using a charcoal grill, the coals are ready when they are about 70 to 80% ash gray during daylight and glowing at night.

- - - - - fold- - - - - - - - - - -

Sloppy Joe Seasoning Mix

1 T. minced onion
1 tsp. green pepper flakes
1 tsp. salt
1 tsp. cornstarch
1/2 tsp. minced garlic

1/4 tsp. dry mustard
1/4 tsp. celery seed
1/4 tsp. chili powder
1/4 tsp. sugar

Combine the above ingredients and stir until well blended. Place in a 3" x 4" ziplock bag and seal.

Attach a gift tag with the directions on how to use the seasoning.

Sloppy Joes

1 pkg. Sloppy Joe Seasoning Mix
1 lb. lean ground beef
1/2 C. water
1 (8 oz.) can tomato sauce

In a medium skillet, brown ground beef over medium-high heat. Drain excess grease. Add Sloppy Joe Seasoning Mix, water and tomato sauce. Bring to a boil. Reduce heat and simmer 10 minutes, stirring occasionally.

Sloppy Joes

1 pkg. Sloppy Joe
   Seasoning Mix
1 lb. lean ground beef

1/2 C. water
1 (8 oz.) can tomato sauce

In a medium skillet, brown ground beef over medium-high heat.
Drain excess grease. Add Sloppy Joe Seasoning Mix, water
and tomato sauce. Bring to a boil. Reduce heat and simmer
10 minutes, stirring occasionally.

★ Cooking Tip ★
To get rid of the odor on your hands after cutting onions try rubbing your fingers on a stainless steel sink.

-- -- -- -- -- -- fold-- -- -- -- -- --

Sloppy Joes

1 pkg. Sloppy Joe
   Seasoning Mix
1 lb. lean ground beef

1/2 C. water
1 (8 oz.) can tomato sauce

In a medium skillet, brown ground beef over medium-high heat.
Drain excess grease. Add Sloppy Joe Seasoning Mix, water
and tomato sauce. Bring to a boil. Reduce heat and simmer
10 minutes, stirring occasionally.

★ Cooking Tip ★

Don't pour grease down your drains as it will plug them. Instead pour your grease into a glass jar with a lid. Keep the jar under your sink for easy access.

- - - - - - - - - - fold - - - - - - - - - -

U. S. of A. Steak Rub Mix

1 T. salt
1 T. plus 1 1/2 tsp. black pepper
1 T. paprika
1 T. minced onion
1 T. minced garlic
1 1/2 tsp. dried oregano
1 T. ground cumin

Combine the above ingredients and stir until well blended. Place in a 3" x 4" ziplock bag and seal.

Attach a gift tag with the directions on how to use the rub.

U. S. of A. Steak Rub

U. S. of A. Steak Rub Mix
Beef

Sprinkle and rub the mix according to taste preferences on both sides of beef before grilling, broiling, baking or frying.

U. S. of A. Steak Rub

U. S. of A. Steak Rub Mix

Beef

Sprinkle and rub the mix according to taste preferences on both sides of beef before grilling, broiling, baking or frying.

★ Grilling Tip ★

To light a charcoal fire, arrange 20 to 30 coals in a pyramid shape. Soak the coals with about 1/2 cup lighter fluid, wait 1 minute for the fluid to soak into the coals and then light with a match.

- - - - - - fold - - - - - -

U. S. of A. Steak Rub

U. S. of A. Steak Rub Mix

Beef

Sprinkle and rub the mix according to taste preferences on both sides of beef before grilling, broiling, baking or frying.

★ Grilling Tip ★

When using a charcoal grill, the coals are ready when they are about 70 to 80% ash gray during daylight and glowing at night.

- - - - - - - fold - - - - - - -

Bayou Blast Rub Mix

2 tsp. salt
1 1/2 tsp. sugar
1 tsp. brown sugar
1 1/2 tsp. black pepper
1 1/2 tsp. celery seed

1 1/2 tsp. paprika
1 1/2 tsp. garlic powder
1 tsp. cayenne pepper
1 tsp. onion powder
1/4 tsp. chili powder

Combine the above ingredients and stir until well blended. Place in a 3" x 4" ziplock bag and seal.

Attach a gift tag with the directions on how to use the rub.

Bayou Blast Rub

Bayou Blast Rub Mix
Fish, seafood, chicken or turkey

Sprinkle and rub the mix according to taste preferences on both sides of fish, seafood, chicken or turkey before grilling, broiling, baking or frying.

Bayou Blast Rub

Bayou Blast Rub Mix
Fish, seafood, chicken or turkey

Sprinkle and rub the mix according to taste preferences on both sides of fish, seafood, chicken or turkey before grilling, broiling, baking or frying.

★ Grilling Tip ★

When grilling, steaks and chops should be turned over when juices appear on their top surface. Peek underneath and make sure the color is golden brown before turning.

- - - - - - - - - fold - - - - - - - - - -

Bayou Blast Rub

Bayou Blast Rub Mix
Fish, seafood, chicken or turkey

Sprinkle and rub the mix according to taste preferences on both sides of fish, seafood, chicken or turkey before grilling, broiling, baking or frying.

★ Grilling Tip ★

When grilling, it is usually best to turn the meat only once. When grilling meat to a medium or greater doneness, use the lid to assist in cooking. This will decrease the cooking time by applying heat to all sides of the meat at once.

- - - - - - fold - - - - - -

Savory Steak Rub Mix

1 T. dried marjoram
1 T. dried basil
2 T. garlic powder
2 T. dried thyme
1 T. dried rosemary
2 1/4 tsp. dried oregano

Combine the above ingredients and stir until well blended. Place in a 3" x 4" ziplock bag and seal.

Attach a gift tag with the directions on how to use the rub.

Savory Steak Rub

Savory Steak Rub Mix
Beef

Sprinkle and rub the mix according to taste preferences on both sides of beef before grilling, broiling, baking or frying.

Savory Steak Rub

Savory Steak Rub Mix
Beef

Sprinkle and rub the mix according to taste preferences on both sides of beef before grilling, broiling, baking or frying.

★ Grilling Tip ★

When grilling steaks or chops, choose cuts that are at least 1 inch thick for tender, moist and tasty steaks and chops.

- - - - fold - - - - - - - - - - - -

Savory Steak Rub

Savory Steak Rub Mix
Beef

Sprinkle and rub the mix according to taste preferences on both sides of beef before grilling, broiling, baking or frying.

★ Broiling Tip ★
When broiling meat, trim excess
fat to prevent flare-ups
in your oven.

- - - - fold - - - - -

Jamaican Jerk Rub Mix

1 1/2 tsp. sugar
1/4 tsp. plus 1/8 tsp.
  onion powder
1/4 tsp. plus 1/8 tsp.
  dried thyme
3/4 tsp. allspice

3/4 tsp. black pepper
1 tsp. cayenne pepper
1 tsp. salt
1/2 tsp. ground nutmeg
1/8 tsp. ground cloves

Combine the above ingredients and stir until well blended. Place in a 3" x 4" ziplock bag and seal.

Attach a gift tag with the directions on how to use the rub.

Jamaican Jerk Rub

Jamaican Jerk Rub Mix
Beef or pork

Sprinkle and rub the mix according to taste preferences on both sides of beef or pork before grilling, broiling, baking or frying.

Jamaican Jerk Rub

Jamaican Jerk Rub Mix
Beef or pork

Sprinkle and rub the mix according to taste preferences on both sides of beef or pork before grilling, broiling, baking or frying.

★ Grilling Tip ★
When grilling, place food about
3/4" apart for even cooking.

- - - - - fold - - - - -

Jamaican Jerk Rub

Jamaican Jerk Rub Mix
Beef or pork

Sprinkle and rub the mix according to taste preferences on both sides of beef or pork before grilling, broiling, baking or frying.

★ Grilling Tip ★

Keep a water bottle handy to mist any flare-ups on charcoal grills. For gas grills, reduce the temperature.

- - - - - fold - - - - -

Hot & Spicy Taco Seasoning Mix

2 tsp. minced onion
1 tsp. salt
1 tsp. chili powder
1/2 tsp. cornstarch
1/2 tsp. crushed dried red pepper
1/2 tsp. minced garlic
1/4 tsp. dried oregano
1/2 tsp. ground cumin

Combine the above ingredients and stir until well blended. Place in a 3" x 4" ziplock bag and seal.

Attach a gift tag with the directions on how to use the seasoning.

Hot & Spicy Taco Meat

1 pkg. Hot & Spicy Taco Seasoning Mix
1 lb. lean ground beef
1/2 C. water

In a medium skillet, brown ground beef over medium-high heat. Drain excess grease. Add water and Hot & Spicy Taco Seasoning Mix. Reduce heat and simmer 10 minutes, stirring occasionally. Makes enough for 8 to 10 tacos.

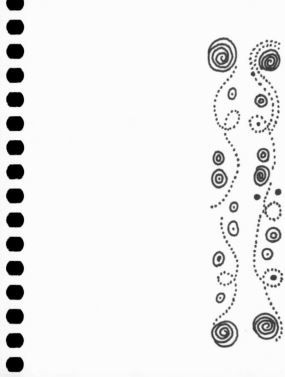

Hot & Spicy Taco Meat

1 pkg. Hot & Spicy Taco Seasoning Mix
1 lb. lean ground beef
1/2 C. water

In a medium skillet, brown ground beef over medium-high heat. Drain excess grease. Add water and Hot & Spicy Taco Seasoning Mix. Reduce heat and simmer 10 minutes, stirring occasionally. Makes enough for 8 to 10 tacos.

★ Cooking Tip ★
Always tear lettuce by hand
instead of cutting with a knife.
This will prevent the edges from
wilting and turning brown.

- - - - - - - - fold - - - - - - - - -

Hot & Spicy Taco Meat

1 pkg. Hot & Spicy Taco Seasoning Mix
1 lb. lean ground beef
1/2 C. water

In a medium skillet, brown ground beef over medium-high heat. Drain excess grease. Add water and Hot & Spicy Taco Seasoning Mix. Reduce heat and simmer 10 minutes, stirring occasionally. Makes enough for 8 to 10 tacos.

★ Cooking Tip ★

To get rid of the odor on your hands after cutting onions try rubbing your fingers on a stainless steel sink.

- - - - - fold - - - - - -

Creole Rub Mix

1 T. plus 3/4 tsp. paprika
1 T. salt
1 T. garlic powder
1 1/2 tsp. black pepper
1 1/2 tsp. cayenne pepper
1 1/2 tsp. dried oregano
1 1/2 tsp. dried thyme

Combine the above ingredients and stir until well blended. Place in a 3" x 4" ziplock bag and seal.

Attach a gift tag with the directions on how to use the rub.

Creole Rub

Creole Rub Mix
Beef, pork, chicken or turkey

Sprinkle and rub the mix according to taste preferences on both sides of beef, pork, chicken or turkey before grilling, broiling, baking or frying.

Creole Rub

Creole Rub Mix
Beef, pork, chicken or turkey

Sprinkle and rub the mix according to taste preferences on both sides of beef, pork, chicken or turkey before grilling, broiling, baking or frying.

★ Grilling Tip ★

When grilling, to determine how hot the fire is, hold your hand above it and start counting. If you have to pull away on the count of one, the fire is very hot, on the count of three, the fire is medium hot and on the count of five, the fire is low.

-----fold-----

Creole Rub

Creole Rub Mix
Beef, pork, chicken or turkey

Sprinkle and rub the mix according to taste preferences on both sides of beef, pork, chicken or turkey before grilling, broiling, baking or frying.

★ Grilling Tip ★

When grilling, chicken and turkey
should be cooked over low heat for
slow, covered cooking.

- - - - - - - fold - - - - - - -